DATE DUE

FEB 0 7 2003

BIRD'S-EYE VIEW OF SAULT STE. MARIE, MICHIGAN.

THE "SOO."

SCENES IN AND ABOUT

SAULT STE. MARIE,

MICHIGAN.

WITH DESCRIPTIVE TEXT.

EDITED BY

C. S. OSBORN.

ISBN-0-912382-30-9

Reprinted 1983

By

 BLACK LETTER PRESS
Grand Rapids, Michigan

Cover art by Robert Nelson

PRINTED BY

KING, FOWLE & KATZ

MILWAUKEE, WIS.

ILLUSTRATED BY

GALL & JURSS

MILWAUKEE, WIS.

INTRODUCTION

Chase Osborn published The "Soo" - Scenes in and About Sault Ste. Marie, Michigan in 1887, a landmark year for the 37-year-old newspaper editor and his newly adopted city. His publication documents a season of high hopes for the north country. Some soon became reality while others remained only dreams.

The man who was to link his own fate with that of Sault Ste. Marie grew up in Huntington County, Indiana, and attended Purdue University for a while, but the bright lights of Chicago beckoned. Osborn had enough of big-city life after a succession of odd jobs and a minor position on the Chicago Tribune. He moved to Wisconsin in 1879 and eventually secured a job with the Milwaukee Signal. Steady advancement in Milwaukee journalism permitted marriage in 1881, and two years later Osborn and his wife moved to Florence, Wisconsin near the Michigan border.

The dynamic young entrepreneur prospered during the next four years. He experienced his first taste of rough and tumble frontier politics, began prospecting for iron in Canada (while incidentally developing a life-long love for the north), and built his little Florence newspaper into a vital operation. In 1887 Osborn sold his holdings in Florence for $10,000., a small fortune in those days, and returned to Milwaukee.

But the lure of the north country proved irresistable. A few months later Osborn took a trip through Michigan's upper peninsula to investigate the region for a Milwaukee investment syndicate. It was then that he first discovered the picturesque old city on the St. Mary's River, and it was love at first sight. That encounter inspired The Soo as an enthusiastic tribute and also determined Osborn's future plans. That fall he purchased, in partnership, the Sault News, a weekly struggling against the rival Sault Democrat. Osborn's fiesty management soon put the News far ahead and he eventually became sole owner.

Chase Osborn's political career also blossomed at the Sault. In 1890 he became the city's Postmaster, in 1895 State Fish and Game Warden, in 1899 State Commissioner of Railroads, in 1908 a Regent of the University of Michigan, and in 1911 Governor of Michigan. Osborn maintained the political philosophy of a progressive throughout his career.

But political success could not satisfy the frenetic Osborn. He roamed the world prospecting for iron and became rich doing it, and he wrote. His bibliography runs to over twenty items including travel narratives, scientific and historical treatises, and an autobiography, The Iron Hunter (1919). Throughout his long and productive life Chase Osborn maintained close ties with the city that caught his eye in 1887.

Sault Ste. Marie attracted other entrepreneurs that year also, because long awaited boom times had finally arrived. The little city had slumbered following the demise of the fur trade which had been the region's chief economic base. While the canal-building excitement of 1853-55 provided a brief influx of business activity, the opening of the canal eliminated the major local employment of portaging goods around the rapids. But news of the coming of the railroads in 1887 brought hoardes of speculators and Sault Ste. Marie awoke to find its streets crowded with strangers, tents pitched everywhere, and choice downtown lots zooming in value a hundred-fold. The long-sought overland link with the world and prosperity for the Sault seemed guaranteed when three separate lines simultaneously snaked their way toward the city. As the Canadian Pacific extended its line from the northeast, the Duluth, South Shore, and Atlantic Railroad connected the region with the south, and the Minneapolis, St. Paul, and Sault Ste. Marie, the "Soo Line," reached out from the west. These railroads would connect at their jointly-financed, 3607-feet-long International Railroad Bridge which, at a cost of $1 million, spanned the St. Mary's River.

The excitement over this railroad-created boom stimulated Chase Osborn to produce The Soo to further promote the city's prospects and to lure potential

investors. It is an excellent example of promotional literature, a genre
noted for hyperbole. Use of this valuable historical document as a research
source requires an important caveat. Internal evidence reveals that it was
published in the summer of 1887, hence many of the visual and textual details
were based on conjecture and prediction. For example, the International
Railroad Bridge, depicted laden with steaming locomotives on page 17, was not
completed until the fall of 1887. Only three of the eleven railroads shown
radiating from the Sault in the map on the rear wrapper ever actually connected.
The sanguine prophecy of a population of 25,000 in three years and eventually
100,000 also proved mistaken. Sault Ste. Marie's population only reached
5760 in 1890, and never came close to 100,000, not on the American side any-
way.

Perhaps the most interesting unexpected development was the power canal.
Its projected date of completion of three years, its purpose to operate water-
powered mills, and even its location as plotted on the map of the city were not
to be. The corporation organized to accomplish the project began work in 1887,
but went bankrupt in two years, with only a portion of the canal blasted out.
In 1898, Francis Clergue, the entrepreneur who stimulated much of the development of the Canadian Sault, restored work on the power canal. Workmen struck
quicksand and the course of the channel was diverted to the north. Finally,
in 1902 the canal and the massive electric power building at its terminus stood
complete. Today the power canal still renders the heart of the city an island
and the 1400-feet-long powerhouse remains an engineering and architectural
marvel.

Caution must be exercised in using any promotional piece as an historical
source. Nevertheless, The Soo provides information not readily available
elsewhere and in particular preserves excellent contemporary graphics.
Engravings such as the birdseye view of the city, old Fort Brady (ca. 1866),
Elmwood (Henry Rowe Schoolcraft's home, now moved to Water Street and under
process of restoration), and the International Railroad Bridge (now existing

as shown only in part) comprise rare views of the period. Illustrations of the
hotels and the highschool document vanished architecture. The ornamental
initial letters beginning each chapter depict contemporary economic activity,
logging, fishing, farming, etc. and are fine examples of an archaic artform.

Original copies of The Soo have become rare collector's items. The
National Union Catalog locates only two American libraries holding the title.
Most of the original printing went the way of similar ephemera, discarded when
the information was no longer relevant. The Black Letter Press has done a
service to modern readers in again making available this souvenir of Sault Ste.
Marie's colorful past.

Larry B. Massie
Western Michigan University

HOUSANDS of eyes have been attracted by the prominent and important location of Sault Ste. Marie, Mich., the hub of the central North, the city with a great future, surrounded, as it is, by many of the greatest natural advantages ever bestowed upon an earthly region. To satisfy a universal demand for information concerning and relating to this Mecca of the manufacturer, the capitalist, the tourist, sportsman and invalid, this little work has been compiled. In the brief time taken to weave the network of facts herein contained, much of importance may have been overlooked, for to do justice to all the attributes of the fortunate Sault would require a volume thrice larger than this. The "Soo" with its key-like location, its grandest water-power in the world, its great locks, the bracing, cooling, exhilarating, healing atmosphere, the solidity that characterizes its present rapid growth, the coming of transcontinental railways, the hundreds of large vessels that pass its great canals daily, the vast local and governmental improvements projected and under way, its unsurpassed agricultural resources, great forest resources, extensive mineral deposits close at hand, splendid school system and local government, elegant churches of many denominations, and many other things that constitute the foundation of a great metropolis, will be a city of 25,000 inhabitants within three years, and its great growth will not cease or diminish.

In the preparation of this pamphlet the compiler was rendered valuable and most efficient assistance by many residents of Sault Ste. Marie, and especial credit for zealous aid is due Messrs. Otto Fowle, William Chandler, Horace M. Oren and Charles R. Stuart, who furnished the greater portion of the contents; their familiarity with the Sault especially qualifying them for their work.

With these few introductory remarks the reader will be led on step by step, commencing with a brief, but clear, concise and complete historical sketch of the oldest point in Michigan, and one of the oldest in the Northwest.

Historical Sketch of Sault Ste. Marie.

Before the white man set foot upon America, the Indian tribes of the Northwest had a favorite place of assembly at the lower end of Lake Superior. Their camping-ground or village was called *Bow-wa-ting* (Falling-Water), and by the earlier inhabitants, *Skiai*. It was situated alongside the rapids, which form a chief feature of the noble stream through which Superior empties itself into Huron, and it was a spot well fitted to attract and draw together the savage tribes. It was one of the best fishing-grounds on the whole chain of lakes, and out of the waters of these rapids the Ojibway Indians have for two centuries gained their chief livelihood. Their right to the use of these fishing-grounds was guaranteed by treaty with the United States, and the tourist of to-day may see the last surviving remnants of this fast vanishing tribe breasting the rapids in their large canoes, and with dextrous casts of their scoop-nets catch the unwary whitefish that served as the chief food-supply of their forefathers.

This Indian village varied in size before the white man came, and as the tribes assembled in greater or less number it sometimes approached the size of a city, and then again was almost abandoned. Its name and location were probably known to the first French commander at Quebec, from the Indian visitors at that post even before any white man had ventured thus far into the interior, and it hardly admits of doubt that it was visited by several French explorers before the Pilgrim Fathers landed on the coast of Massachusetts. The traditions of the Ojibways confirm this statement, they being to the effect that several white men came among them before the "Black-gowns," or Jesuits. The latter first looked upon Sault Ste. Marie, or as they, or the explorers who had preceded them, designated it in honor of the younger brother of the French King, Saut du Gaston, in 1641.

In this year Father Charles Raymbault and Isaac Jogues visited the village at the rapids. They came from the Mission station established among the Huron Indians near the lower end of the Georgian Bay. This Mission station was the first established west of Quebec, and had met with a reasonable degree of success. Raymbault and Jogues were sent to explore with a view to extending the field of their labors, and coasting along the Georgian Bay and picking their way through the island-bound channels of the St. Mary's River, they drew up their boats at the Indian village at the foot of the rapids and advanced among the wonder-stricken natives, waving the cross, the symbol of their faith.

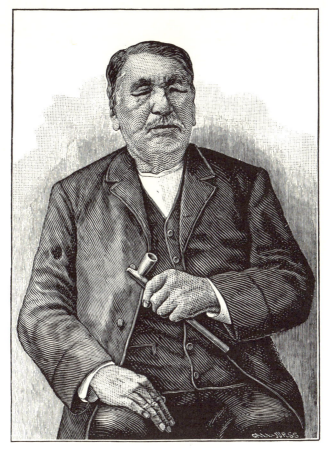

OLD OJIBWAY, CHIEF OF THE CHIPPEWAS.

"And ne'er till lost is mem'ry's power,
  Shall we forget the thrilling hour
  Of our swift passage down the 'Soo,'
  In 'Indian John's' light birch canoe."

They met with a friendly reception, and left with the intention of returning the following summer and establishing a permanent Mission station. But misfortune struck them and their fellow-workers unannounced. In returning to Quebec, Jogues fell captive into the hands of the Iroquois, and after a series of adventures bordering upon the marvelous, escaped to France, but returned voluntarily among his former captors and while endeavoring to persuade them to peace was treacherously slain. Raymbault died of consumption at Quebec the next year, and the Mission stations among the Hurons were destroyed by the Iroquois, and their inmates were burned at the stake.

For a number of years after these tragic events the Jesuit cause waned in the Northwest, but the French trader and courier-de-bois, as reckless and venturesome as the most savage of the Indians, did not cease to sally forth from Quebec and Montreal to the most remote points of the interior, and the priests did not follow far behind. In 1660 Father Mesnard passed by the rapids into Lake Superior, and coasted along the southern shore to Portage Lake, along the shore of which he became lost, and perished. Five years elapsed and he was followed by Father Allouez, who passed on to the western end of Lake Superior, and on one of the islands of the Choquamegon Bay put up a small chapel and Mission station, a building which was the first permanent habitation of a white man erected in the great Northwest of the United States. This was at the site of what subsequently became known among the voyageurs as La Pointe.

The second habitation was at Saut du Gaston, or, as it was thereafter called, Sault Ste. Marie. Claude Dablon and James Marquette arrived in 1668, and carrying out the cherished plan of Jogues and Raymbault, founded a Mission station among the Sauters (Indians at the rapids). These two small buildings, over two hundred years ago, were all that betokened the coming of the white man into that great empire forming at present the central and western part of the United States. Sault Ste. Marie enjoys the distinction of being the oldest town in Michigan, and, outside of La Pointe and a few scattered Spanish settlements in the Southwest, the oldest point west of the Alleghany Mountains.

From 1668 to 1689 the Mission station at Sault Ste. Marie flourished. It was successively occupied by Jesuits, who by their indefatigable labors in exploring, and their illustrious martyrdoms, have won imperishable names in the annals of American history. Nearly if not all had some connection, at some time or other, with the station at Sault Ste. Marie. The acknowledged importance of this Mission is seen by the fact that in 1671 it was made the scene of a pageant, designed to

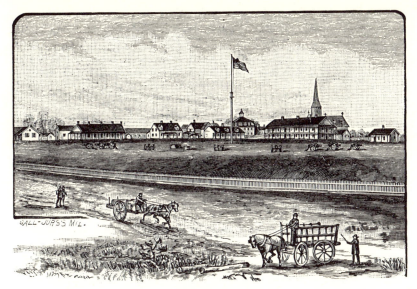

OLD FORT BRADY.

win the allegiance of the Indian tribes of the Northwest. A great council was called at Sault Ste. Marie, and in the presence of the chiefs and representatives of fourteen tribes, Sieur de St. Lusson, a lieutenant of the Governor General of French Canada, with a pomp and display well calculated to excite the admiration and awe of his savage spectators, took possession, in the name of his most illustrious sire, the Grand Monarque of France, of all the lands extending from Montreal to the South Sea. A cross was planted and the shield of France suspended from a cedar post. It was the formal announcement of the claims which France laid to the interior of the new continent, a claim which she proceeded to make good by exploration and settlement, and which was only wrested from her by a bloody war.

The exact location of the Mission house of Dablon and Marquette is not known, although it is generally supposed to be near the northeast corner of the grounds now occupied by Fort Brady and not far distant from the handsome Catholic church, which is a prominent object to those approaching Sault Ste. Marie from almost any direction. The building is described as having been a small log chapel and house, enclosed within a square of pine and cedar pickets twelve feet high. We read of an instance of rather rough usage to these buildings in 1674. An Indian was killed by some visiting Sioux, and the latter having been set upon by the residents of the village, and being in fear of their lives, sought refuge in the Mission house. Louis Bohesme, the blacksmith attached to the Mission, in order to dislodge them, fired a cannon into the building until its occupants were killed and the house quite thoroughly demolished. In 1689 the Mission station was abandoned, owing to the growing importance of Mackinac as a fur-trading center and the necessity of centralizing their efforts. Sault Ste. Marie continued, however, as a station of the traders, although of minor importance.

It was not until the middle of the next century that anything of importance occurred relating to Sault Ste. Marie. In 1750 the Canadian Governor, Jonquiere, gave to his nephew, Captain de Bonne, and Louis Lagardeur (Chevalier de Repentigny), a Canadian soldier of fortune, a grant of land bordering upon the rapids and river of the St. Mary's for six leagues, and extending a like distance into the interior. The grant was made upon the condition that the grantees should erect a palisade fort at the rapids. This was built, was 110 feet square and contained three houses. A farm was cleared in connection with the post, and it was stocked with cattle. It had been intended to raise Indian corn in large quantities, but this agricultural experiment failed. The chief object of the post was to prevent the Indians of Lake Superior from coming down to Oswego, New York, where they received presents from the English, and were being seduced from their allegiance to the French. In this connection it might be well to say that the representatives and heirs of Bonne and Repentigny laid claim to the site of Sault Ste. Marie and the land granted to them by Jonquiere, and their claim was so far recognized by Congress that in 1860 an act was passed allowing them to institute proceedings in the United States Courts to prove their rights. In this they failed, the United States Court rendering a decision adverse to their claim.

The location of this fort was near the northeast corner of what is now Fort Brady, and directly in the rear of what is now the present Catholic school. It was substantially constructed with a palisade fifteen feet high. It was hardly completed before the French and Indian war came on, and Repentigny and Bonne both left the post in charge of one of their employes, Jean Baptiste Cadotte (Cadeau), who was destined to play an important part in the subsequent history of the Lake Superior region. Upon the surrender of Mackinac to the British in 1762, a detachment under Lieutenant Jeanette proceeded to take possession of the post at the Sault. He found Cadotte in possession, and meeting with no opposition, he took up his quarters in the abandoned garrison. His stay was short, however, as in December of that year fire destroyed the whole station, and Cadotte was left in undisputed possession. He proceeded to put himself on good terms with his Indian neighbors, and he received a grant from them of a large tract of land, composing the present site of the city. During the Pontiac conspiracy, Cadotte was friendly to the British and prevented the Indians at Sault Ste. Marie from joining in the massacre at Mackinac. His wife, who was a woman of unusual force of character, prevented the recapture of Alexander Henry, the only Englishman who survived the massacre at old Mackinac and escaped to tell the tale of disaster. Mrs. Cadotte brought Henry to the Sault, and through gratitude for his rescue he offered a business partnership to Cadotte in the fur and Indian trading business. This was carried on for several years with mutual profit and advantage. He died in 1803.

Cadotte had two sons, Jean Baptiste and Michael, both of whom engaged in the fur trade and rendered important service to the Northwest, and other fur companies that were gradually monopolizing this industry. The former died at Sault Ste. Marie, and he has numerous descendants living at this place.

Another resident of Sault Ste. Marie was John Johnston, an Irishman of good education and refined manners, whose fortune threw him among the Indians of Lake Superior. He married a daughter of Waube-geig, a noted chief of La Pointe, and for many years he was the chief resident of Sault Ste. Marie, and dealt out hospitality from his residence, still standing, in a manner that does credit to his memory. The chief industry of this period was fur-trading. The Northwest Fur Company was a consolidation of several smaller companies, among them that of Henry and Cadotte. This was established in 1807. It continued with various fortunes until 1819, when it was pushed to the wall by its more powerful rival, the Hudson Bay Fur Company, and a consolidation was effected. These companies made Sault Ste. Marie one of their chief stations and the Hudson Bay Company erected extensive buildings and warehouses on the Canadian side of the rapids. The buildings are standing to-day and are an object of interest to the tourists and pleasure-seekers who throng at Sault Ste. Marie every summer.

In 1802 the British post was re-established at Sault Ste. Marie,

ostensibly on the Canadian side, but in reality the American influence
had hardly begun to assert itself on its proper side of the river. In
1820, when Governor Cass visited the Sault, he found the British flag
flying on the American side of the river, and the inhabitants came near
mobbing him for pulling it down and replacing it with the stars and
stripes. During the war of 1812 a band was organized at Sault Ste.
Marie, under the leadership of John Johnston, to go to the assistance of
the British at Mackinac, who were hard pressed by the Americans. The

OLD U. S. INDIAN AGENCY. (A LANDMARK.)

latter had their revenge, however. The schooner Scorpion, under com-
mand of Lieut. D. Turner, of the United States Navy, during the last
week of July, 1814, landed a force of infantry under Major Holmes, at
the Sault. Johnston and his company escaped down the Hay Lake
channel. The troops burned the trading-post of the Northwest Fur
Company and the huts of those who had been disloyal. They also
attempted to take a schooner, called the Perseverance, used by the company, through the rapids, but this was not a success and the boat and
its cargo were burned. The visit of Governor Lewis Cass to Sault Ste.
Marie, already referred to, was a notable one. He gained important

cessions from the Indians and proceeded to voyage the entire length of Lake Superior, and sought the long-looked-for source of the Mississippi. He recognized the necessity of establishing a military post at the Sault, and on his recommendation Gen. Hugh Brady was sent, in 1822, to found the garrison, which has gone by the name of its founder, Fort Brady.

Governor Cass, on his trip, was accompanied by a young man, who thereafter filled a most important part in the history of Sault Ste. Marie, and who, in those lines of investigation relating to the history and condition of the aborigines of North America, took first rank among American scholars. Reference is had to Henry R. Schoolcraft. In 1822 he was appointed Indian agent at Sault Ste. Marie, and for many years he occupied the old Indian agency residence, which is still occupied and exists as an object of historical interest. He married a daughter of John Johnston, already referred to. Schoolcraft had his residence at Sault Ste. Marie for many years, and did most of his literary work here. He represented Chippewa County in the Territorial Legislature, and did more than any other one man to advance the interests of the section of country in which he lived. In 1828 Chippewa County was organized, embracing the entire northern half of the Upper Peninsula, and extending toward the west until it took in the greater part of what was subsequently Northern Wisconsin. It was a county of magnificent dimensions, and Sault Ste. Marie became the county seat. Up to this date Sault Ste. Marie was but little else than a fur-trading center. After this the British Fur Company, the Astor, and then the American Fur Company had it as one of their headquarters. As a center of the fur trade, however, Mackinac dwarfed all surrounding posts, and it was not until an appreciation of the mineral wealth of the Lake Superior region began to dawn upon the American public, that Sault Ste. Marie assumed a position of any real importance. It is unnecessary to recount the discovery and development of the mineral resources of the Upper Peninsula. The geological survey of Dr. Houghton and other eminent scientists confirmed the traditions of the existence of copper and iron in unusual quantities. These men were followed by an eager band of explorers and speculators, and from 1841 to 1855 the influx into the Upper Peninsula rivaled the great rush to California on the discovery of gold. This state of affairs added materially to the importance and prosperity of Sault Ste. Marie. There was no ship canal at that time

and all the outside supplies for the upper lake had to be unloaded at
the foot of the rapids and transferred over a portage road to the head
of the rapids and re-shipped at great expense. Even the vessels which
were sailing on Lake Superior had been handed out and dragged around
the rapids in the same way. The transfer and supply business became
the great industry, and as the mining fever developed and the Lake
Superior district began to boast of its few scattered but permanent settlements, it seemed as if Sault Ste. Marie was destined to be the central
and chief city of this region. A weekly newspaper was started, published, however, only through the summer months. This paper was the

LOCKS — CLOSED.

direct progenitor of the Marquette Mining Journal. Its editor was J. V.
Brown, who took an active part in securing the legislation which resulted
in the building of the St. Mary's Falls ship canal. The portage trade,
in the very nature of things, could not last. The demands of Lake
Superior were too urgent to admit of the delay and harassment incident
to this method of transfer, and the construction of a ship canal around
the rapids became a practical problem which demanded a speedy
solution. Governor Mason in 1837, in his first message, advised the
building of such a canal, and during the same year a survey was made
for that purpose. In 1838 an appropriation bill was passed by the Legislature and in the following year the contractors commenced the work.

Much to their surprise the military authorities considered the work an infringement upon the rights of the General Government, and an armed force from Fort Brady drove the contractors off the ground. This put a quietus to the work for several years, although the advocates of the measure did not cease to urge it upon the attention of the State Legislature and Congress. In 1852, however, the latter passed a bill appropriating 750,000 acres of land to aid in the construction of a canal. In 1853 the Legislature authorized the commencement of the work. The contract was let to construct two consecutive locks 350 feet long, 70 feet wide, and with a depth of 13 feet of water, and proper canal approaches.

LOCKS — OPEN.

These were the old State locks, now about to be torn out and replaced by a single lock which, in its dimensions and capacity, will be the largest in the world. On the 21st of May, 1855, this canal was completed at an actual cost of $999,802.46. It resulted in adding Lake Superior to that system of water-ways which is the pride and the chief commercial feature of the northern border. From the opening of this canal until 1870 there is little to be said regarding Sault Ste. Marie. In the building of this canal it lost much of its commercial prestige, and these years witnessed a decadence instead of an advance. In 1870, however, an impetus was given to its growth by the commencement of a new lock south of that built by the State. This was conducted under the superintendence of the General Government, and it was finished in 1881. This lock is 515 feet long, 80 feet wide in the chamber and 60 feet in the gates. It will admit vessels drawing 16 feet of water, accommodating the largest boats in the lake trade.. The same year that it was opened the State of Michigan transferred the old locks to the United States, and they both passed under one management. Some statistics as to the shipping passing through this canal will be given in another connection. Suffice it to say, there is probably no other commercial highway in the history of the world that can present an equal showing.

At present the old city is enjoying a legitimate revival, which was bound to come in the natural course of progress and the development of the Northwestern United States. In a year or two it will be a greater railway highway even than it is a water-way, if such is possible, and the utilization of its natural advantages, for which every preparation is making, will make it a most important manufacturing and commercial center of large proportions.

How to Get to the Sault.

Best of all is the route by way of the splendid passenger steamers that leave Buffalo and Detroit daily (Sunday excepted) for Sault Ste. Marie and Duluth, another line leaving Chicago every other day for the same points. The journey is delightful, and is not attended with half the danger incident to an ordinary railroad trip. Those who have less time or have no relish for the trip by water, can take the cars to Mackinaw, Cheboygan, Marquette, or St. Ignace ; thence by reliable boats to the Sault. These boats leave the places mentioned daily. Their course is near shore and is by daylight all the way, reaching the Sault just in time for the passengers to hear the sun-down gun from Fort Brady. After, and perhaps before, the close of this season several all-rail routes will terminate at the Sault, making it easily accessible by rail from all points.

NONE but those who have lived in the heated cities and malarial atmospheres of the parallels of Cincinnati, St. Louis and Chicago, and have tried the delightful transition to this pure, health-giving, delightful atmosphere, can begin to realize or appreciate the benefits such a change will bring. Not until one comprehends the geographical position of Sault Ste. Marie, sees it situated in the extreme east of a vast peninsula, the southern shores of which are laved by Lakes Huron and Michigan, the noble river St. Mary, with its roaring rapids, bounding it on the north and east, and that grandest and greatest of inland waters, *Gitchee Gumee* (Lake Superior), on the northwest; that north, northeast and northwest beyond these waters stretch the wilds of the British possessions, hundreds and hundreds of miles, to Hudson's Bay, to Labrador, to the North Pole, if needs be, almost totally uninhabited, except by a few settlers along the St. Mary's River, and fewer still along the line of the Canadian Pacific, which winds, with rocky bed, far north of Lake Superior, can the absolute purity of the atmosphere of Sault Ste. Marie be realized. Let the winds blow from north, east, south or west; when they fan the Sault they are as pure as a wide expanse of pure water and unbroken wilderness of pines and balsams can make them. This pure atmosphere, laden with ozone and with balsamic odors; supplemented by the delicious drinking water, fresh from the cool depths of Lake Superior, are never-failing restoratives to the victims of catarrh, asthma, hay-fever, sunstroke, fever and ague, and the kindred diseases so prevalent in the heated cities and miasma-burdened country farther south.

The health-giving power of this atmosphere is no matter of speculation; its efficacy has been demonstrated time and time again. Every season brings familiar faces and strange ones, too, eager to escape their dreaded foe, hay-fever, and the fact that the strange faces become familiar by repeated visits, is proof of the efficacy of the cure. It is not to the

INTERNATIONAL RAILWAY BRIDGE.

afflicted alone that we would recommend the Sault as a resort. It is a prime place for pleasure-seekers. A recreative, enjoyable time may be had. What more pleasurable experience can the over-worked, over-heated, worn-out citizen of our pent-up cities, who is daily tortured by burning pavements and scorching sun, and robbed of sleep at night by sultry, contaminated air, look forward to than a refreshing trip on one of the magnificent steamers, through the cool waters of the north?—a trip that from its inception is health-giving and pleasant, and the last sixty miles up as beautiful and grand a river as sends its waters towards the ocean. The beautiful river St. Mary, the Hudson of the North, even as the Hudson is justly styled the Rhine of America, has an entire length of about seventy-five miles, and varies in width from a half mile at Garden River and the Neebish (Indian for tea, or boiling water), to several miles at the small lakes, which constitute a considerable portion of its length.

The Canadian shore, rock-bound by precipitous bluffs, lacks only the ruined villas and castles of the Fatherland to make it a veritable Rhine. To the lover of nature, historic landmarks are supplied by the hut and wigwam of the native Indian, whose primitive abodes dot the sands and rocks along the shores. Of much greater interest to the tourist are the remnants and ruins of old forts and posts, built as frontier defenses in days long agone, which stretch their gaunt arms, whitened and crumbling by long exposure, towards the blue sky. Each could a tale unfold if, speech-inspired, they might talk, and each has its history. The ruins of old Fort St. Joseph, on St. Joseph Island, Canada side, can be seen quite plainly from the boat, as well as many other points of historic interest, touched upon more fully in another place. On the American side the land is more level, and covered by forests, slowly giving way to the pioneer farmers, whose clearings and log-cabins are forerunners of cultivated farms to follow in good time. Looking up Hay Lake from the Neebish can be seen the smoke of the dredges at work for Uncle Sam, making a new channel through Hay Lake, shortening the present channel about twelve miles. Work has been prosecuted on this canal several years, and at the present rate of appropriation several years more will transpire before the completion of this necessary and important work.

Owing to the tortuous course of the river and the narrow channel in many places, it is impossible, until the completion of Hay Lake channel, for the boats to run at night. Detour passage, at the mouth of the river, is therefore reached in the morning. Thenceforward the delighted tourist has before him a panorama of charming landscapes, until the foaming rapids, spires and towers of the future metropolis of the North, terminate as delightful a boat-ride as can be had on the continent.

When arrived at the Sault, what can be enjoyed? First, a pure atmosphere filled with ozone, that to breathe makes one strong and, alas for the landlord, hungry, too. Next, a sure and sweet night's rest ; for however warm the sun at mid-day, evening brings its cool breeze, and refreshing sleep is enjoyed under a generous supply of blankets.

Over and above other Northern resorts sharing a similar atmosphere, the Sault is pre-eminent in having a hundred things to amuse and gratify. From the balconies of our large hotels the delighted visitor and old inhabitant, too—for of this the oldest inhabitant never tires—can watch the roaring, dashing, foaming rapids, more pleasurable to many than the rapids and falls of Niagara, with real, live Indians in the foreground who, in their light canoes dancing in the swift current, skillfully "scoop" with their dip-nets the shining whitefish from its element. There is pleasure in witnessing this primitive mode of fishing, and pleasure, too, in the thought that the fish you will have for dinner, supper and breakfast, too, if you choose, is fresh ; that it is not the stale article of the southern markets that has been packed and repacked and shipped for hundreds of miles until it is fresh only in name. The Sault whitefish goes into the frying-pan, as the Indian says, " a-kicking."

These Indian boatmen are serviceable in contributing to a sport which, for dash and exhilarating effect, cannot be excelled—"shooting the rapids"—an experience never to be missed and always to be remembered, as the Chicago man said after taking the ride down the rapids :

"I wouldn't have missed that for a hundred dollars."

On being asked to repeat it, he said he wouldn't go down again for a thousand.

It is a trip having much more apparent than real danger. The Indian pilots have spent their entire lives on and about the rapids, know almost every rock in them, and so skillful have they become in the use of their paddles, in guiding the frail canoes in the proper channels, that not one accident is recorded.

The boats, carrying a commerce greater than passes the Suez Canal, continually passing just in the front of the visitor as he sits on his hotel piazza, or walks the walls of the greatest locks in the world, are a source of unfailing interest and instruction.

The locks in the foreground, the foaming rapids, the Canadian islands beyond, with rocks and evergreens striving for place, the old Hudson Bay Company's trading-post, and, rising in the background, the Canadian hills, emerald and bold, make a landscape well worth coming to see, and many times enjoyed when here.

During the season there are almost innumerable excursions radiating from the Sault, one or more almost daily, and much to be enjoyed — to

SWINGING GUARD GATE AT ENTRANCE TO CANAL.

Bruce Mines, to Point Aux Pins, to Garden River, to Little Rapids, to Shingwauk, and last, but not least, to "go fishing." The lover of this sport can have his fondest wish realized, for the speckled trout, the genuine brook beauties, are abundant and grow to magnificent proportions. The gamey pickerel and bass, and fierce muskalonge also abound in their season, while herring, perch and whitefish are taken from the locks and canal by wholesale. Men, women and the unconquerable small boy enjoy a unity of interest in picking the shad-fly from each other's clothes and baiting their hooks, sure to catch a fish, but the small boy, of course, taking the lion's share.

HE citizens of Sault Ste. Marie realize that a healthful, steady growth of their city depends most of all upon its becoming a manufacturing center. To this destiny Nature has contributed everything that the most exacting could ask. Situated on the river, coal is brought by cheap water transportation direct from lower lake ports. But a few miles away, either by rail or water, are the great iron and copper mines of the Upper Peninsula, while all around within easy reach are thousands of acres of timber awaiting the woodsman's ax and the charcoal burner, all pointing to this as an excellent point for the location and operation of blast furnaces, rolling mills and iron manufactories of every description, while no better point for shipment of manufactured articles can be found.

First, and above all other things, for becoming a manufacturing city, Sault Ste. Marie depends upon its unrivaled

Water Power.

The magnificent river St. Mary, nearly a mile wide as it passes this point, in the course of three-quarters of a mile falls eighteen feet from the level of Lake Superior, which is but a few miles above. Government engineers have estimated the discharge to be 90,780 cubic feet of water per second. Nature offers no obstructions to the use of this power. On the contrary, a ledge of rock coming to the surface of the ground at the head of the rapids, running at right angles to the river and reaching back to the highlands, renders it safe and practicable to construct a canal from the river above the rapids to a point below, without the danger of Lake Superior washing away any safeguard which man, without this ledge of rocks, might have been forced to provide for the security of the city below. The Government canal, locks and docks, about a mile and a quarter in length, render it necessary to construct a canal not less than three miles in length, to which the formation of the ground in its course offers no obstruction.

For many years capitalists and engineers have looked upon this stupendous power as sure to be utilized some time. Protracted litigation over the right-of-way for the canal, and lack of railroad communication, deferred the enterprise, until it was finally left for citizens of the Sault to carry it into effect. The question of utilizing the rapids of the St. Mary as a motive power came to a crisis in 1885, when it was decided to construct a system of water-works for the supply of the city. The citizens had voted for the loan of the necessary funds with the understanding that the pumps should be operated by water-power, thus calling the attention of the world to the inexhaustible power at hand. The City Council seemed to have different ideas, and were about closing negotiations for steam-pumping machinery, when an almost unanimous uprising of the citizens called a halt. A citizens' committee was appointed and authorized to employ a competent hydraulic engineer to submit plans and estimates. Fearing the amount loaned by the city would be insufficient, a corporation was formed with sufficient capital pledged to supplement the public funds and carry out the work. The Council became impatient and the day before the matured plans and specifications for utilization of the water-power came, showing the scheme to be feasible, the Council closed the contracts for steam machinery.

Though forestalled in their original plans this little corporation of citizens, on seeing the magnitude and importance of the work, were loth to relinquish the enterprise, on the success of which they deemed the future of the city depended. The company re-organized under the State law, was increased by a few additional members, means secured, and negotiations for the right-of-way pushed with vigor. At the same time steps were taken to secure the capital necessary to complete the work.

In May, 1887, the entire right-of-way was secured, and immediately thereafter a contract was entered into between the corporation and a syndicate of Western capitalists, who agree to construct the canal, security being given that one hundred thousand dollars at least will be expended in the work of construction, within eighteen months from the time of execution of the contract, and the entire work to be completed within three years.

The proposed canal, upon which work has been actively commenced, runs parallel with the river and about half a mile distant. The purpose is to construct a canal one hundred feet wide, carrying a depth of fifteen feet of water. This, with a fall of eighteen and one-half feet, will supply a power practically inexhaustible.

The City Council, shortly after its organization, granted the company, with proper restrictions and conditions, the right to cross all streets with the main canal and to run lateral canals or penstocks to the river, thus enabling mills and factories to be located on the river, to which easy access can be had by boats on one side and railroad trains on the other.

One of the most valuable features of this power is that it will be unfailing and invariable. While the Mississippi for a few months each year furnishes an abundant power, the remainder of the year forces the Minneapolis mills to run with but part capacity, or supplement the water-power with steam-power. Lake Superior, the mill pond of the St. Mary's Falls Water Power Company, has no appreciable rise and fall, and St. Mary's River never varies to exceed nine inches from the mean height, and is most often highest in the dryest weather. With this grand power utilized, the possibilities of Sault Ste. Marie cannot be realized. The magnitude of this vast power can perhaps be best shown by comparison with a few of the most important water-powers of the country.

The flow of the Connecticut River at Holyoke, Mass., is about 5,000 cubic feet per second, making the nominal capacity of the stream 30,000 horse-power, according to a printed statement made by the Holyoke Water Power Company. This is, by the same authority, claimed to be equal to the capacity of the water-powers of Lowell and Lawrence combined. The maximum capacity of the water-power at Minneapolis is estimated at 30,000 horse-power. In all these places the power varies in a vast degree. At certain seasons of the year the torrents dash over the gates and waste-weirs, amounting to naught to the manufacturers, but requiring the expenditure of vast sums of money for the protection of the dams and canals. At other seasons of the year the water is so low that, in order to keep their mills and factories running, the owners are compelled to maintain expensive steam plants as auxiliaries to the water-power. At each of these points the power seems to be growing less each year.

Take, then, the full power of the places named, and the aggregate

BOAT HOUSE.

does not exceed 90,000 horse-power, while the unvarying flow of the St. Mary's River, with the 32,000 square miles of Lake Superior as a reservoir, furnishes an estimated power of 725,000 horse-power, or *eight* times the aggregate power of the places named. With a small portion of this power harnessed for use, Sault Ste. Marie bids fair to rival Minneapolis in her great milling enterprises. The Sault will depend on the same territory as Minneapolis for her supply of wheat, with equal if not better facilities for obtaining it. The Minneapolis mills grind largely in transit. The Sault will have equal railroad facilities for grinding in transit, with the inestimable advantage of water transportation in addition, for the grain-laden vessels from Duluth and other Lake Superior ports must needs pass through the Sault and stop to be locked down from the level of Lake Superior to that of Michigan and Huron.

The wheat-laden trains from the West can as cheaply discharge their freights at Sault Ste. Marie and reload their flour for the Eastern markets, as to discharge the grain at Minneapolis, for Minneapolis must send her flour through the Sault to the Eastern markets, or take the much longer route around by Chicago ; while vessels carrying the millions of bushels of grain annually shipped from Duluth, passing by the mills of Sault Ste. Marie, will have the opportunity of there discharging their cargoes, and without unmooring, reload with flour for Buffalo and Montreal, and when the Canadian canals are deepened and enlarged, the cargo taken on at Sault Ste. Marie can be discharged, without reloading, at Liverpool, Bremen, or any other European port.

Fisheries.

The proximity of Lakes Superior and Huron, and the numerous small lakes forming no inconsiderable part of St. Mary's River, make the Sault important in her fisheries. Lake Superior whitefish are noted in the markets for their excellence, while trout (lake and brook), pickerel, pike and muskalonge, bass and sturgeon, are shipped in abundance. The trade is now important and is fast increasing.

Boat Supplies.

At present a growing branch of trade is dealing in boat supplies. Few boats pass either way that do not lay in new supplies at Sault Ste. Marie. This trade grows apace with the increase of lake traffic, and has become an important feature.

HIPPEWA County, of which Sault Ste. Marie is the capital, bounded on the east by the St. Mary's River, extends from Lake Superior on the north, to Lake Huron on the south, and includes several large and numerous small islands in the St. Mary's River. The extreme length of the county east and west is about 100 miles. The entire county, except where cleared by settlers and forest fires, is covered by heavy forest, including all the varieties of timber usually found in this latitude. Extensive lumber operations are continually carried on, and the shore line from Lake Superior down to Lake Huron is dotted by large saw mills, fast converting the pine into lumber for the Southern markets. Interspersed with the pine and hemlock throughout the county are extensive tracts and belts of excellent hardwood. Running west from Waiskai River, the entire length of the county is a belt of hardwood from sixteen to twenty miles wide, composed of beech, birch and maple. The maple is of superior quality, running largely to bird's-eye, and grows large and thrifty. The birch is remarkable for its richness in color, and grows very plentiful. This hardwood is found in smaller tracts on most of the islands and throughout the mainland. The lowlands and river bottoms are thickly grown with a heavy growth of poplar and spruce, while cedar is abundant. In providing means for cheap transportation of these woods to the Sault, Nature has again granted her helping hand. This timber, as a rule, is within easy reach of lake and river, the combined shore line of which comprises an extent of fully 360 miles, all within a radius of seventy miles from the Sault, while the shore line of the Canadian side is of equal length and abundantly timbered. The timber, banked on lake and river, can be loaded

HOTEL IROQUOIS.

on flat boats and towed to its destination at a nominal expense. Sault Ste. Marie, then, has the essentials for extensive

Pulp Mills.

Unfailing water-power, and poplar and spruce in abundance, can be delivered to these mills at a nominal cost.

The convenient forests of birch, maple and pine, with cheap power, bespeak for the Sault an important industry in the manufacture of

Furniture and Wooden Ware

of every description. With the opening of the Hennepin canal, the tropical woods and rich veneers, by the all-water route, can be laid down at the Sault cheaper than at Grand Rapids and many of the Eastern furniture manufacturing points.

Fine Writing Papers.

The pure, soft water of Lake Superior, with the abundant water-power, make it possible and practicable to manufacture here the best quality of writing paper, an industry in which all attempts of Western manufacturers have failed for lack of proper quality of water.

Railroads.

The coming winter of 1887-8 is to be one of hardship to the " old inhabitant " of the Sault, in depriving him of a pastime with which he has whiled away many a long winter. No sooner had winter placed its icy embargo on ship and steamer, and news came with the mail, once in a while, sixty-five miles overland from Point St. Ignace during these later days, and formerly three hundred miles by dog-train from Bay City, than the ancient " Sooites " gathered in groups around red-hot stoves and built railroads without number, an interminable network from everywhere to everywhere, and all leading to the Sault. These railroads were built and operated with vigor until the first boat rounded Top-sail Island, when these railroads vanished in thin air, or were laid away for the next winter's use. Alas! this delightful bubble-blowing, this time of air-castle building, is past. Railroad building, with chain and coil, with pick and shovel, is inaugurated. Two railroads from the West and two from the East, are in actual course of construction, running a race to see which shall first reach the Sault, while the construction of the International bridge across the rapids is being pushed with energy, and will be in operation before the close of navigation.

The Duluth, South Shore & Atlantic connects at Duluth with the entire railroad system of that place, and, availing itself of many miles now in operation, proposes to fill in the gap and have trains running to the Sault by September, 1887.

The Minneapolis, Sault Ste. Marie & Atlantic connects at Minneapolis with all roads centering there. With more miles to build than the Duluth road, it still advertises to have trains running into the Sault by January, 1888. This line, under another name, is being extended westward from Minneapolis into Dakota, penetrating the richest wheat-growing sections of that vast region.

On the Canadian side railroad building to the Sault is being pushed with all energy. The branch of the Canadian Pacific from Algoma Mills to the Sault, ninety miles in length, will be completed early the present season, while the Grand Trunk is using every endeavor to be on hand for a co-partnership in the International bridge. Other lines of railroads to the Sault are proposed, the preliminary surveys for which in several cases have been made, all tending to designate Sault Ste. Marie as a future great railroad center.

A glance at a map of the United States and Canada will show the almost perfect air line through the Sault from Minneapolis, St. Paul and Duluth to Montreal, to Boston, Portland, and other Eastern seaboards.

Measurement shows the line from Minneapolis, St. Paul and Duluth *via* Sault Ste. Marie to New York, to be over 200 miles shorter than any line in operation around by Chicago ; to Boston about 300 miles shorter ; to Portland 350 miles, and to Montreal about 400 miles shorter, a saving in distance so marked as to insure a heavy traffic over these lines that has formerly gone by way of Chicago. Sault Ste. Marie, being the necessary terminus of the American lines, will be the natural location of round-houses, machine-shops and division headquarters, adding materially to the prosperity of the place.

The improvement of the carrying facilities by rail and water will tend to make freights to the Sault cheap, while the almost perfect communications West and North, and its far removal from other large cities, bespeak for the Sault a prominence in the wholesale trade.

Government Work.

The fast increasing commerce which passes the Sault demonstrates that the time is not far distant when the present lock, the largest in the world, will be wholly inadequate. The present canal, which, at the time the present lock was constructed, was deepened from eleven to sixteen feet, is found to be too shallow for many vessels now in the carrying trade. It is therefore proposed by the Government to construct a new lock of double the capacity of the present lock, and to deepen the canal to a depth of twenty-one feet. Work is in progress for the construction of the new lock, which will be prosecuted with as much vigor as the appropriations of Congress will permit.

The lock in course of construction is to be 800 feet long inside of the gates, and 100 feet wide, with gates full width of the lock chamber. The canal, when deepened to twenty-one feet, will require the movable dam to be altered to suit that depth. A pier is to be constructed in front of Fort Brady and the north pier extended 1,000 feet. The completion of this work will require the expenditure of something over four million dollars.

The work on Hay Lake channel, on which the Government has

already expended $295,000, will have cost when completed a total of $1,185,000.

At a recent session of Congress a bill was passed for the sale of the present site of Fort Brady, the purchase of a new site in some other portion of the town, and the erection of a post accommodating four companies of soldiers, the present post comprising but two companies. The bill referred to appropriates $120,000 for this work. A new site has been purchased on an eminence about one-half mile from the ship canal.

MICHIGAN EXCHANGE.

The Government work at the Sault, *now in progress*, will require at least $5,200,000 to complete.

The Board of Fortifications for the United States, in its report of January, 1886, in speaking of places on the great lakes which should be fortified, says :

"The canal at Sault Ste. Marie would also demand a fort to prevent it from destruction."

Hence it is to be expected when the Government decides to construct a system of coast defenses, that Sault Ste. Marie will come in for its share.

This vast expenditure of money for Government work, while it will not prove a permanent support for the town, will still be continued through a period of several years, and will greatly assist the town to prosperity during the time required in the construction of the Water Power canal, after which the Sault will take her place among the prominent manufacturing and commercial cities of the country.

Mineral Resources.

While Chippewa County lays no claim to mineral resources beyond the existence of large deposits of good foundation-stone, the Canadian region, for a radius of twenty-five miles from the Sault, and directly tributary to it, forms one vast, unexplored region, indicating great richness in iron, silver and copper. With the incoming of railroads this region will be thoroughly explored and rapidly developed, giving birth to a great mining industry, which will be supplied from Sault Ste. Marie, and will be a field of trade of great magnitude, if the dovolopmonto aro equal to prospects at present shown by mineral indications at many places.

Climate.

The climate of this locality does not differ materially from that of Minnesota and Dakota. Winter sets in usually about the first of December, but steady cold weather does not begin until January, and usually ends in March. During these months snow falls to an average depth of about three feet. In these months, also, is experienced the coldest weather, the mercury sometimes dropping to twenty degrees below zero, and occasionally even to forty degrees or more. During extreme cold weather there is, however, little or no wind, and the atmosphere is dry, consequently one does not suffer more from the cold when the mercury is twenty degrees below zero, than is endured in Detroit or Chicago when the mercury is six or eight degrees above, there being no dampness in the atmosphere. In 1886 the highest temperature was ninety-three degrees above, and the lowest thirty-nine degrees below zero. The mean temperature for the year was thirty-eight degrees. The Summers here are delightful, and the heat is seldom or never oppressive. The mornings and evenings are exceedingly refreshing, and the nights always cool enough to sleep with delicious comfort.

HE soil of Chippewa County is rich and strong, and is therefore well adapted to agricultural purposes. The principal crops, and those which are produced to the best advantage, are : Spring and Winter wheat, oats, barley, peas, hay, potatoes and all kinds of vegetables. With industry and intelligent cultivation, the farmer never fails to obtain good crops of all kinds. Winter wheat does not "winter-kill," as it remains well covered with snow, which forms a complete protection from Fall, until a time in the Spring when all danger of freezing is over. It ripens considerably earlier than Spring wheat and can be safely harvested. There is no doubt that Chippewa County, and in fact the greater portion of the entire Upper Peninsula, will in a few years become as famous for wheat culture as Minnesota and Dakota are now. In the early years of the settlement of this county its farmers had the courage to compete, for several seasons, at the State Fairs. The exhibits included Winter and Spring wheat, oats, barley, potatoes and peas. Both varieties of wheat, and the potatoes and peas, received first premiums on every occasion. The displays attracted great attention. Our Lower Peninsula neighbors had always supposed that this was an unproductive and unimportant region, but, to their astonishment, we bore off the palm in competition with the products of their most favored localities.

There is a large percentage of lime in the soil, and the more it is worked the better is the crop. The average yield of Winter wheat is about twenty-five bushels per acre ; Spring wheat, eighteen bushels ; oats, forty bushels ; peas, thirty-five to forty bushels. This is a conservative estimate. Insects destructive to crops are unknown. Potatoes yield large crops. Hay averages from one and one-half to two and one-half tons per acre, and is of unusually good quality. The county is adapted for stock raising, especially sheep, as hay, oats and roots are large and sure crops. The Wintry atmosphere being dry and very pure, and the summers cool, sheep are always healthy.

Another industry which will become largely profitable as soon as undertaken, is celery culture. There are large tracts along the river and lake shores, of rich black muck and loam, just such soil as that along the Kalamazoo River, where the famous celery farms are located.

In fact, this region presents endless advantages and innumerable opportunities to farmers. This fact is fast becoming known and is stimulating the very rapid settlement of the county in all directions by a thrifty class of Canadian, Scotch and English farmers. These hardy tillers of the soil bring with them experience, intelligence and vigor, which are the very elements necessary to make Chippewa County a veritable garden from one end to the other. The soil possesses lasting qualities, as evidenced by farms which have been tilled for forty years and are as productive to-day as when first cleared. The system of county roads is far above the average, and each year brings with it great improvements in this important direction. In this brief space the half cannot be told. Suffice it to say that Chippewa County, and in fact, all that portion of the Upper Peninsula and Northern Wisconsin directly tributary to Sault Ste. Marie, and as yet so undeveloped, contains a vast acreage of as rich farming land as the sun ever kissed. Civilization, which goes hand in hand with the railroad, will turn this into a great growing section, which will supply our rapidly growing city with all the necessaries produced on the farm, and also furnish the materials for turning many factory wheels.

Fruit Culture.

Fruit culture has not been widely attempted in Chippewa County, but enough is known to warrant the direct assertion that with proper methods of selecting, setting out and caring for fruit trees, their culture would be attended with full success. The hardier varieties of Russian apples, some kinds of cherries and pears, and even plums, can be made to yield a good and sure crop here, while Siberian crab-apples thrive without extra care. As for small fruits, almost an endless variety are indigenous to this locality. So extremely favorable is the condition of our soil and climate that they attain the very highest degree of excellence and perfection. They are also exceedingly prolific, and the greatest success has rewarded the efforts of all who have engaged in their cultivation. This is particularly true of the raspberry, blackberry, currant and strawberry—the first named and last abounding all about us in a wild state. This can also be said of whortleberries. In the vicinity of Whitefish Point, above here, cranberry culture is extensively engaged in. Even now the gathering and shipping of raspberries, cranberries and blueberries constitute a large and growing industry in the Autumn. The Indians bring them to the city in quantities, and hundreds of bushels are shipped to the Detroit and Chicago markets. So, it will be seen, this region presents opportunities for fruit culture which, once

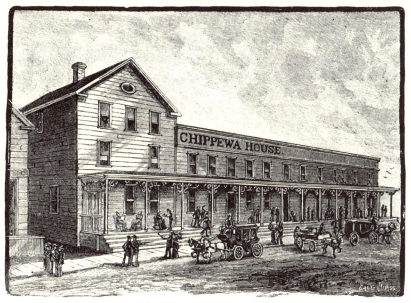

CHIPPEWA HOUSE. (A LANDMARK.)

properly utilized, will make it independent of foreign supply and give good returns to those engaged in it.

The Building Boom.

At present it is next to impossible for new-comers to procure a house to live in or a place to transact business. Tenting is much resorted to just now. Dozens of substantial brick business places are in course of construction, and at least one thousand new dwellings will be erected this season. A prominent characteristic of the building improvements is their permanency. People have not come to the Sault for a day, nor for a year, but fully realizing the future of the city, they have come to stay, and are doing everything in the most substantial manner. Fire limits have been created by the local government, and everything is being done to prevent disastrous fires, which in other rapidly-growing towns have proved so destructive.

Banking Facilities.

At present Sault Ste. Marie has three well-organized banks, sufficient to supply the demand in this line at present, although another is talked of. Those at present doing business are the Sault Savings Bank Loan and Trust Co., the First National Bank and the Sault Ste. Marie National Bank.

Hotel Facilities.

The city is quite well supplied with hotels, the four more prominent being the Hotel Iroquois, the Michigan Exchange, the Chippewa House and the Hotel Superior. The former two are new hotels, and the Iroquois is adding one hundred rooms to its already large capacity.

Natural Gas.

It has been asserted that the strata underlying Sault Ste. Marie are identical with those of Findlay, Ohio, and other points in the natural gas region. Enterprising citizens are about to organize to make a test for gas, and if successful the Sault manufacturing advantages will be greatly enhanced.

Cost of Living.

The cost of living at Sault Ste. Marie does not differ materially from other points. This matter has been carefully investigated, and the statement can be intelligently and truthfully made that it does not cost more to live at the Sault than at other places of the same size.

Water Supply.

The water supply of the city is obtained from St. Mary's River or direct from Lake Superior, through the means of excellent water-works, which are being extended over the city as fast as energetic work renders it possible. The water is clear, pure and healthful.

Location of the City.

A more pleasant, healthful or eligible location for a city than that possessed by Sault Ste. Marie could not be found. It is high, level and commanding, admitting of excellent drainage, and so shaped as to allow streets to be laid out in regular order, with proper respect for squares and angles. Improvements of lots can be made at a reasonable cost. The business portion of the city is located conveniently to the docks, and, taken as a whole, the location is unsurpassed. As for scenic natural beauty, Nature has treated the vicinity of Sault Ste. Marie with lavish hand.

City Discipline.

Sault Ste. Marie is an orderly, order-loving city. It is well policed, both day and night. The public peace is rarely or never disturbed, saloons are kept under strict regulations and compelled to close at a seasonable hour, and brawls and fights are almost unheard of. In fact, the city is controlled by a large law-abiding, order-loving element, which has always been in the majority and always will be. Although the city is growing rapidly and is constantly crowded with eager investors and their concomitant attendants, the discipline is equal to that of any other city and far surpasses that of larger places.

Corporation Laws of Michigan.

The State of Michigan has dealt liberally with its manufacturing and mining corporations, and in return there has been invested in its borders the capital of the Eastern states and the countries of Europe. None other in the Union has done more to invite outside capital, and fair and liberal laws relative to the formation and regulation of corporations has been the rule in Michigan. The general provisions concerning manufacturing companies will be found in Chapter 124, of Howell's Annotated Statutes of Michigan. Its provisions are simple. Organization is effected by merely filing articles of association in the office of the Secretary of State. As to taxation, under the present law companies and corporations are on the same footing as ordinary individuals. Manufacturing establishments desiring to use the great natural advantages that are to be found at Sault Ste. Marie, will find in the laws of Michigan, facilities for organization and advantages to be found in few other states.

School System.

Sault Ste. Marie is fully abreast of the other cities of Michigan, noted throughout the United States for their admirable school systems. It has a handsome brick high-school building, erected in 1879 at a cost of $15,000, two ward-school buildings, and others are being added as fast as necessity requires. There is an excellent corps of teachers, and the younger generation at Sault Ste. Marie have all the advantages of education that they would have in any of the larger cities of the West. The first commencement exercises of the Sault Ste. Marie high-school were held June 17th, 1887, there being nine graduates, all fitted for entrance into the University. It is intended to make the school system, as has been done in other Michigan towns, supplementary to the University, and properly subordinate in the school system which has made Michigan so pre-eminent.

HE village of Sault Ste. Marie was incorporated in 1845, but this organization was not kept up, and there was a re-incorporation of the village in 1870. This not proving very satisfactory, the village was again re-incorporated in 1879, by a special act of the Legislature. Owing to the rapidly increasing growth of the village and the need for a more elaborate system of government, a city charter was prepared this Spring, which has been lately adopted by the Legislature and received the approval of the Governor. The charter is admirably drawn, and by those who have examined it pronounced one of the best that could have been devised for the new metropolis of the North. It will take effect in April, 1888, and the first charter election will be held on the first Monday of that month. The present local government is, in the main, satisfactory. The men who have been at the head of affairs have been progressive, and fully awake to the interests of the village, and under their administration most of the local improvements that are being made were originated. In 1885 there was a system of water-works planned, which was completed in the following year. The pump-house is located near the head of the ship canal, and mains are quite well distributed throughout the business and residence portions of the town. The system was put in at a cost of $40,000, for which amount the city has issued bonds payable in twenty years. During the present spring a complete system of sewerage was devised by Edward C. Burns, a well-known sewer engineer of Jamestown, N. Y. The plan embraces a complete sewerage of the town, and has been approved by the local authorities. The work will begin at once. The plan suggested by Mr. Burns is to flush the sewers from the bay above the rapids, their outlet being at the extreme east end of the village. This gives an ample fall, and in utilizing the various natural advantages, Mr. Burns has devised one of the most complete and satisfactory systems that has ever been planned, and one that will stand the test of use in time.

The bonded indebtedness of Sault Ste. Marie is $45,000, which, considering the size of the place, value of the improvements already made, prospects of growth and the other attendant advantages, is extremely light. The indebtedness of the county does not exceed $20,000. This amount is being yearly decreased, and was incurred in the erection of the various county buildings, in which Chippewa County can take genuine pride. In a new locality indebtedness of this character cannot be considered a disadvantage, for it is the only proper means of obtaining the necessary public improvements, and where the indebtedness is as low as in this place and there are so many improvements to show for it, it is not to the discredit of the locality.

Taxation.

For state and municipal purposes taxes in Sault Ste. Marie are proportionately as moderate as in any locality in Michigan. Improvements have had to be made and will have to be made, which will demand a considerable outlay of money, and this may for a time make the rate of taxation somewhat higher than it would otherwise be, but business men and manufacturing enterprises will have no cause to complain by reason of excessive taxation at Sault Ste. Marie.   There is not a state in the Union that is as economically administered as Michigan, and the economy that is manifested in its state affairs is, in an equal degree, characteristic of its subordinate municipalities.

Local Improvements.

There has been a standing prediction throughout the Upper Peninsula that the first street cars to be run in that portion of Michigan, would be upon the streets of Sault Ste. Marie. This prediction will be verified within a period of not less than six months, as a

Street Car Company

has lately been organized, been granted a franchise by the city, and has put itself under bonds to begin active work on its street car line within six months, and complete at least two miles of its track on or before eighteen months from the 23d day of May, 1887.

A Gas Company,

headed by the Hon. D. B. Henderson, of Dubuque, Ia., has lately organized and been granted the privilege of laying its pipe in the streets, and it has also agreed to have its work in operation within less than a year from the present date.

An Electric Light Company

has also been formed, and in this connection it might be well to state that the unlimited power furnished by the rapids and the water-power canal, will cause electricity to be furnished for the purpose of illumination, at a cost far less than it can be supplied in any other city in the United States. It is safe to predict that Sault Ste. Marie will be the best lighted and best watered city in the country. The place has had a good deal to contend with in its streets, it being an old French town, and the characteristics of such a town were stamped upon its face. The municipal authorities, however, have been persevering in their efforts to correct these irregularities, and are beginning to make the streets of a proper form and width. Since the great interest with reference to real estate in this vicinity last Winter, there have been plats made of most all the property lying around and in the vicinity of the city. This has been laid out in streets and avenues in regular form, and in a manner that will assure to the future resident of Sault Ste. Marie the satisfaction of living in one of the best laid-out towns in the country.

Newspapers.

Two weekly newspapers are at present published at Sault Ste. Marie. They keep fully abreast of the times, and are indices of the growth and prosperity of their home. They have secured the United and Associated Press franchises, and within a short time will be published as dailies.

Churches.

In its origin a Mission station, Sault Ste. Marie has always been a center for religious instruction and fellowship. The Baptist and Methodist denominations had Mission stations established here early in the present century, while the Catholics date their occupation to a period over 200 years ago. The different denominations having churches in the city at present are the Baptists, Methodists, Presbyterians, Catholics, and the Congregationalists are just completing an elegant new house of worship. Families coming to the Sault for residence will find all of those church and other advantages, which they may have left in their former places of residence.

Means of Entertainment.

The city has just completed a handsome municipal building, in which there is a large public hall, used for and suitable for theatre and all other public entertainments. A $30,000 opera house is classed as among the probabilities of the near future, and other enterprises of like character are on foot. During the Winters the ordinary Northern Winter sports are provided for, and a toboggan club, which has now been organized for two years, has erected and kept in proper order a toboggan-slide, which is said to be the longest and best equipped in the entire Northwest.

The Boating Club.

Among the Summer amusements boating is chief, and the Falls City Boat Club, an organization formed in 1883, has erected a handsome boathouse and supplied it with a complete outfit of boats, which may be used by members of the club. The terms of membership are easy, and this institution is one in which the city takes considerable pride.

Benevolent Societies and Organizations.

The Masons, Knights of Pythias, Odd Fellows, Ancient Order of Hibernians, and several other organizations of like character have lodges at Sault Ste. Marie, and their society halls are as well equipped as any in the Upper Peninsula of Michigan. In fact, Sault Ste. Marie embraces, even now, all the advantages to be found in large cities, and new residents will miss none of the comforts, conveniences or advantages which they may have left behind them.

Some Investors.

Among the moneyed men who have invested here and are improving or about to develop their property, are: Charles A. Greeley, Nashua, Ia.; Thos. W. Burdick, banker, Decorah, Ia.; James H. Easton, banker, Decorah, Ia.; Frank P. Searle, banker, St. Cloud, Minn.; A. B. Wilgus, real estate, St. Paul; O. F. Sherwood, real estate, St. Paul; William Hendricks, real estate, St. Paul; J. N. Rogers, real estate, St. Paul; N. F. Bickle, banker, St. Paul; S. H. Thompson, capitalist, St. Paul; W. C. Bennett, capitalist, St. Paul; M. Haas, capitalist, St. Paul; John Spry Lumber Co., lumber, Chicago; Frank Perry, lumber, Bay Mills, Mich.; R. D. Perry, lumber, Bay Mills, Mich.; Chas. L. Bonner, manufacturer, Winona, Minn.; George Martin, Naperville, Ill.; Levitt K. Merrill, attorney, St. Paul; Clarence B. Wardle, capitalist, St. Paul; George O. Severance, capitalist, St. Paul; J. H. Everett, St. Ignace, Mich.; B. T. Bailey, manufacturer, Charles City, Ia.; T. E. Bryan, treasurer, Charles City, Ia.; Edward Billings, banker, Charles City, Ia.; J. E. Stowell, grain merchant, Ada, Minn.; Thorp Bros., grain merchants, Ada, Minn.; H. B. DeGood, corn merchant, Minneapolis; John C. Cabanne, real estate, St. Paul; A. B. Bushnell, attorney, St. Paul; R. E. Watson, capitalist, St. Paul; Walter C. Teter, real estate, St. Paul; Leopold & Austrian, vessel owners, Chicago; Arthur Hill, lumber, Saginaw; Chas. A. Supe, merchant, Bay City, Mich.; Lieut. Lea Febiger, U. S. Army; F. W. Solomon, real estate, Chicago; The Minneapolis and Sault Ste. Marie Land and Improvement Co., composed of Minneapolis capitalists, at the head of whom is Hon. W. D. Washburn; besides which are a great many other capitalists interested in the different enterprises of the new city.

The Water-Power Syndicate.

The Water-Power Syndicate, which is the heaviest investor, and which will do the most to build up the town, is composed of Cargill Bros., grain and elevator owners, La Crosse, Wis.; Robt. Eliot, grain merchant, Milwaukee; Rosenbaum Bros., grain merchants, Chicago; Foss, Strong & Co., grain merchants, Chicago; "Diamond Joe" Reynolds, McGregor, Ia.; Bassett, Hunting & Co., grain and elevators,

McGregor, Ia.; Jos. Clark, lumber, La Crosse, Wis.; J. G. Stradley, Cresco, Ia.; W. A. Stowell, grain merchant, Minneapolis; Frank W. Commons, grain merchant, Minneapolis, Minn.; J. B. Canterbury, La Crosse, Wis. This great syndicate has already invested over $500,000 in real estate and right-of-way in Sault Ste. Marie.

Sault Real Estate Values.

Real estate values are comparatively low. Acre property is changing hands and can be obtained at about $75 near the city limits, to $400 and $600 in almost the center of the town. Desirable business lots range from $75 to $250 per foot and residence lots at from $20 to $500 each. Very often property is offered at prices which would not be unreasonable in any country village of about 5,000 inhabitants, and which will pay a desirable interest on the investment from the date of investment, and as there will be a population of 25,000 here within three years, increasing then very rapidly, probably to 100,000, the profits on the principal can easily be estimated. In fact, there is no property here but that by the erection of appropriate buildings, a good interest would be derived from the date of completion. There is an erroneous idea abroad that property here is too high. If it did not command some value it would indeed be worthless, but when investments can be made which will be doubled, trebled and quadrupled, it would take the genius of a Cato to find fault with them.

A Building Association.

A strong building association, with a capital stock of $1,000,000, has been organized by local and outside capitalists, having for its object the same advantages usually offered by such associations. This association will aid the poor, but industrious, to obtain homes of their own, on the small-payment, long-time plan, with low interest. This is the same method that has proved such a blessing to the working-class of all large cities.

A Natural Center.

Sault Ste. Marie is remote from other large centers of trade and population, which is a factor in its favor not easily over-estimated, and not to be lost sight of. Holding such a key-like position, as it does, to a large and rapidly-developing territory, it is bound to be a great distributing point. The "Soo" is the hub to a large wheel of territory, which can revolve around no other axis. This territory is rich in manifold resources, and its chief city, Sault Ste. Marie, will be populous and wealthy. To this end it has entered upon a phenomenal growth. If you want to invest in and grow up with a town that will be a great city in a few years, visit Sault Ste. Marie and look into its manifold advantages, which cannot be exaggerated.